P9-AQC-967

Holidays & Festivals

HALLOWEEN

Robin May

Rourke Enterprises, Inc.
Vero Beach, Florida 32964

6148480

Holidays and Festivals

Buddhist Festivals
Christmas
Easter
Halloween
Hindu Festivals

Jewish Festivals
Muslim Festivals
New Year
Sikh Festivals
Thanksgiving and Harvest

Text © 1989 Rourke Enterprises, Inc.
PO Box 3328, Vero Beach, Florida 32964.

All rights reserved. No part of this book may be reproduced or utilized in any form
or by any means, electronic or mechanical, including photocopying and recording,
or by any information storage and retrieval system without permission in writing from
the publisher.

Library in Congress Cataloging-in-Publication Data

May, Robin.
    Halloween / Robin May.
      p. cm. – (Holidays & festivals)
    Bibliography: p.
    Includes index.
    Summary: Describes the origins of Halloween celebrations and
traditions and how they differ throughout the world.
    ISBN 0-86592-983-1
     1. Halloween–Juvenile literature.   [1. Halloween.]   I.Title.]
    II. Series: Holidays and festivals.
    GT4965.M28 1989
394.2'683–dc 19   88-15657
                                        CIP
                                        AC

Printed in Italy by Tipolitografia G. Canale & C. S.p.A. - Turin

Contents

ℛ475939

Halloween Celebrations

A Very Old festival

Halloween! A time for games, fun and fortune-telling, for ghosts stories and making mischief. At Halloween on October 31, millions of people celebrate a very old festival indeed.

For centuries, people believed that Halloween was a night when witches walked – or flew! – and ghosts and spirits were on the loose. Ordinary folk also believed they could see into the future.

For hundreds of years, the thought of witches has frightened people at Halloween.

Today, many people say that Halloween is just an excuse for a good time. After all, who believes in ghosts and magic nowadays?

In fact, many people do. Yet what makes Halloween so special is its long and colorful history. For all the fun and games, it is part of the story of Britain, Ireland and northern France – part of their 2,000-year-old Celtic past. It belongs to North America, too.

Halloween was originally known as the Festival of the Dead, and it had a strong hold on our Celtic and Saxon ancestors. The Church wanted to break this hold, and to do this called it All Hallows' Eve. Hallow means holy, holy man or saint. This later became Halloween, and the Church made November 1 All Saints' Day. But Halloween was never really a Christian festival, and we do not think of it that way today, either.

Halloween has always been a good excuse to play games and have fun.

A Night of Fun and Frights

Some of the fun of Halloween comes from scaring people or being scared by them, but there is more fun than fear in these activities. In the past, though, Halloween activities were often more frightening. For example, 150 years ago in Scotland, youngsters attacked each other's bonfires with sticks and stones to wreck them. Back then, fires played a big part in Halloween.

Fortune-telling was also important to Halloween. Girls stuck apple seeds on their cheeks. Each seed stood for a sweetheart, and as the seeds fell off, the girl knew which sweethearts to get rid of. Soon only one was left. While waiting for the seeds to fall off, she said:

Pippin, Pippin, I stick thee there,
That that is true, thou mayest declare!

A frightening fifteenth-century picture of witches, devils and evil spirits.

6

Meanwhile, the chances were that a nearby cottage door would be unlatched and inside there would be food on the table. The family put it there for their dead relatives to enjoy. They believed their relatives would visit them. The fire would be alight so that the spirits could warm themselves. This was supposed to make the coming winter easier for the spirits to bear.

Ordinary people believed that terrors came out that night. One horrible Welsh phantom was the tailless black sow, which was expected to appear after everyone had enjoyed themselves around a hilltop bonfire. When the fire was dying, everyone ran down the hill shouting "May the tailless black sow take the hindmost!"

Meanwhile in Hertfordshire, England, and elsewhere, lanterns were kept burning all night in order to keep foul fiends out, just in case.

In Scotland, youngsters used to wreck each other's bonfires with sticks and stones.

7

Once upon a Time

The Festival of Samhain

When the Romans first came to Britain in 55 B.C., they found people called Celts there. The Celts had two seasons: winter, from November to May, and summer. And to them, the first day of November was not only the first day of winter, it was also the first day of the new year. This the Celts celebrated with the festival of Samhain (or Samhuin), their New Year's Eve. (Samhain means "summer's end" in Celtic.) The Celts also had a spring festival called Beltane, our May Day.

The Celts gave thanks for their harvest on Samhain, but it was also a festival of the dead. It was a time when vegetation was dying. Life and

The Celts were mainly farmers, raising cattle and working the land.

8

crops would return early in the summer.

There was feasting at Samhain and also human sacrifice. Food was left for the dead, because everyone believed that they would return on that night! Everyone was frightened and tried to avoid the visiting ghosts. Sometimes they ate the food that the ghosts were meant to share. This is commemorated at Knutsford in Cheshire, England, where "soul" cakes are eaten by candlelight – light that is supposed to guide the spirits back to their old homes.

The Celts tried to make peace with each other at Samhain, just as we try to at Christmas. Later, in the 800s, the Church made All Saints' Day – November 1 – a Christian Samhain, and All Souls' Day – November 2 – a day to remember the dead. All Hallows' Eve was an attempt to Christianize Halloween, but it failed.

The Celts sacrificed humans at the festival of Samhain.

9

Hallow Tide

Though Halloween is not itself a true Christian festival, the Church, as we have seen, became involved with the pagan feast. As far back as the seventh century, there was a special feast for all the saints in heaven on May 13. The Church switched this feast to November 1 in 834, calling it All Saints' Day.

So it came about that on November 1 the saints of the Church were suitably celebrated, and still are.

Over 150 years later, in 988, it was decided that

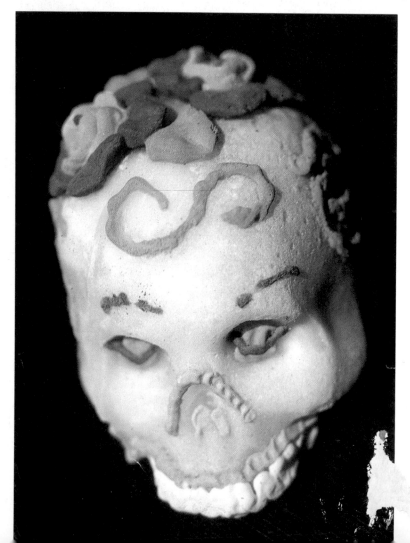

Sugar skulls like this one are eaten on All Souls' Day in Mexico.

Christians honor the dead at Hallow Tide.

November 2 would be known as All Souls' Day. On this day, the Church remembered all faithful Christians who have died. It is a day when Roman Catholics offer prayer for those still in purgatory who have not yet been blessed by reaching heaven and God.

Thus in the Church calendar, Halloween – All Hallows' Eve – directly precedes two holy days, All Saints' Day and All Souls' Day. Together these two days are called Hallow Tide (tide means time). Christianity honored the dead – certainly more reverentially than the lively festival of Halloween.

But Halloween itself has become a non-religious occasion, and, at least in North America, only those who are actively involved in churches are aware of Hallow Tide.

The "Little People"

Once, the Celts believed that the people who had inhabited Britain before them were the "little people." The little people were supposed to know all about herbs and poisons in a way that their enemies did not and could vanish into the landscape without a trace. It is not surprising, then, that the Celts came to believe that the little people had magical powers. They also thought that Samhain and Midsummer Eve were big nights for the little people.

The Romans, who conquered the Celts, also came to believe that the countryside was full of

A seventeenth-century picture of the little people dancing in a circle.

the little people. The Romans did not feel that all these mysterious folk were hostile, but they did think that the little people had the power to frighten them.

Being practical people, the Romans also combined two of their festivals with the Celtic Samhain. "Feralia" honored the dead in late October, while "Pomona" honored the goddess of trees and fruit. That may well be the reason why apples are connected with Halloween.

People believed in the existence of the little people long after the Romans left Britain, and even today there are people who believe that the little people exist. Many of those enchanted folk from fairy tales stem from these little people, including such favorites as fairies and goblins.

Pomona (center) was the Roman goddess of trees and fruit.

Fairy Places

If one of our ancestors offered another one a trip to fairyland, he or she would think that the other was mad! No night was more dangerous than Halloween, for it was believed that one could be snatched away forever by fairies.

A seventeenth-century register of death has three people frightened to death by fairies, and one led into a horsepond by a will-o'-the-wisp.

As for being snatched from the real world to fairyland – a hazard in ancient Scotland, so they say – there was a chance of getting back. The victim had to recite the right spell at the correct spot.

There were even routines for getting to fairyland. If you circled a certain Scottish hill nine times between dusk and dawn on Halloween, it was said that a door in the hill would open. Enter it, and you would be in fairyland.

It was believed that you could enter fairyland by circling a certain Scottish hill nine times on Halloween.

There are many superstitions about fairies. Anyone unlucky enough to get a visit from a fairy when moving from one house to another was in real trouble. Bad luck was inevitable. However, even worse was for an area to lose its fairy population altogether. To guard against this it was necessary to have a good supply of food handy just in case the fairy folk needed it.

And on Halloween, fairies would appear in the homes of people whose ancestors had chased them away many years earlier.

An old music sheet with fairy dancers on the cover.

Witches, Spells and Fortune-telling

When Witches Walked

Witches were greatly feared by nearly everyone less than 300 years ago, and by some people in our own century. At Halloween, people believed they were at their wicked worst, and fires blazed across the countryside to frighten them and other evil spirits away.

In Scotland, a country steeped in Halloween traditions, there is a custom of burning a model witch on a bonfire at Halloween. All over the country, people used to light bonfires to keep spirits of evil away. Scottish children in Aberdeenshire used to go around collecting fuel for the bonfires and shouting: "Gie's a peat t'burn the witches" ("Give us peat to burn the witches!"). The fires were supposed to burn the witches as they flew over them on their broomsticks.

Queen Victoria used to enjoy Halloween at Balmoral Castle in Scotland. There, an effigy of a witch was tried and condemned to be burned. This stuffed figure, which had been brought forward to the sound of bagpipes, represented

Witches are supposed to be at their wicked worst at Halloween.

16

all the bad things that had happened to the local clan. The evils, supposedly, were burned with it.

At Balmoral, the witch was not a real person, but a dummy. Yet tales exist of real women being burned to death because they were suspected of witchcraft. Many of these deaths probably took place on October 31.

Four accused witches being "examined." In times past, convicted witches were put to death.

17

Accused witches were often strapped into a ducking stool – if they floated in the water, they were guilty; if they sank and drowned, they were innocent.

"Leeting" the Witches

A high spot in the anti-witch war took place every year at Halloween at Malkin Tower. This was the Forest of Pendle in Lancashire, England. The locals were convinced that witches met there on the big night, so they started a ceremony known as "leeting" or "lating" the witches, meaning lighting them.

They believed that if they carried a large lighted candle between 11 p.m. and midnight near the tower, and the flame stayed steady, the witches' power would vanish. But woe betide the idle carrier who let his light go out – or was it blown out by a witch? – as this was supposed to mean bad luck. Naturally, it needed a brave man to carry a candle.

Scotland's great poet, Robert Burns, described in *Tam o' Shanter* what happened to Tam at Halloween. Full of drink, he came upon witches and warlocks (male witches) at a church, with the devil himself playing the bagpipes! The sight of one "winsome" – pretty – witch among them made Tam shout for joy. At once, all the lights went out and the witches came after him. He just managed to escape but his poor horse lost its tail to a witch.

Tam had ridden halfway across a bridge, which made him safe. The horse's tail had been in the wrong half!

The wood from the mountain ash tree, which is called rowan, is believed to protect people from witches. Supposedly, one wave of rowan at even the wickedest witch and you would be safe.

There is an ancient rhyme to remind us of this belief. "Nag" is a small horse or pony:

If your whip stock's made of rowan
Your nag may ride through any town.

Tam o' Shanter and the witches he saw dancing in the church.

Magic Fire

For our ancestors, fire meant warmth and light. It also spelled magic. It could help to ensure that the sun would return after the winter.

All over the world there were – and are – fire festivals and, as we have seen, Halloween is one of them. And Halloween fires mean far more than ordinary bonfires.

At Halloween, Lancashire people used to burn straw on the prongs of pitchforks and pray for their dead loved ones.

Stories about the devil and evil doings were told at Halloween.

A sacred flame was thought to protect ordinary folk from the powers of darkness. At Halloween in Ireland in ancient times, the druid leaders met at a place called Tlachtga. This was near the holy hill of Tara, the ancient seat of Irish kings. At Halloween, every fire in Ireland was meant to be put out and later lit again from the holy fire of Tlachtga. Then and only then could all be sure of a safe future.

As late as the last century, farmers in Britain would walk with their families around their fields holding torches. These they had lit from Halloween bonfires. As long as they did this, so they believed, their crops would grow and their cattle would produce calves.

Early in this century in Lancashire, England, Halloween was called Teanday from "tan," the Celtic word for light and fire. Straw was burned on the prongs of pitchforks, as all prayed for their dead loved ones.

Naturally, another reason for bonfires at Halloween was for clearing up garbage and dead vegetation. Farmers knew that ash was good for their soil. Many people believed that light would also help souls in purgatory – the place where the Roman Catholic Church says dead people are forced to stay until their souls are purged of their sins. When they are purged, it is taught, they can enter paradise. To this day, there are several "purgatory fields" in northern England, and one is even called Purgatory.

A Torch against Evil

Torches and torch-light processions have always been associated with Halloween, especially in Scotland and Wales.

Farmers in Britain used to carry torches through their property at Halloween and recite spells to protect it through the grim winter months. Children used to hold torches in front of a mirror in a dark room on the big night and say:

Dingle dingle dowsie, that cat's in the well
The dog's away to Berwick to buy a new bell.

An eighteenth-century picture of people and evil creatures going to the Sabbat – a meeting of the devils and witches.

No one now has any idea why they said this!

In Scotland and Wales, "hallow fire" was a tradition that must have depressed many people. A group of people built a fire, and each person marked a stone and threw it into the fire. The next day, everyone returned to the scene. If a person's stone was still there, all would be well; a damaged or missing stone meant that the thrower would not live to see the next hallow fire. In some places, the stones were put around the edge of the fire. If any of the stones had moved in the night or been damaged, the "owner" was thought to be doomed.

Torch-light processions have long been associated with Halloween.

Husband or Wife Hunting

In olden times, many girls expected to find out what their marriage prospects were at Halloween. So did young men.

A well-loved way of finding out the future was to bake a cake with a ring, a thimble and a coin in it. The coin meant riches for the finder; the ring meant wedding bells sounding; but the poor thimble finder would never be wed. Of course he or she could hastily bake another cake!

There is an old British story of six farm workers who sat in a circle around a pitchfork, which was sunk in the ground with a clean shirt hanging on it. Each man thought that his loved one would appear before midnight and take the shirt away, proving that her love was true. No one came, so the men decided that none of their girlfriends were true to them.

Also at Halloween, some girls would go into

Many people believed that Halloween was the right time to consult a fortune-teller.

With luck, a girl would see her future husband after sowing hemp seeds.

plowed land and begin sowing hemp seed. "Hemp seed I sow, who will my husband be, let him come and mow," they recited. Then they would look over their left shoulder and, with any luck, there would be their future husband.

Some girls in northern England had a different way of finding out who their husbands might be on Halloween night. Without speaking, a young girl would prepare the dough for a bread called a bannock. Then she put the bannock on the baking griddle and went to bed, still in silence. That night, in her dreams, she might see her future husband turning the bannock on the griddle.

In the Scottish Highlands, girls used to find out the size and shape of their future husbands by drawing cabbages while blind folded.

More on Marriage

A hundred years ago, also in England, teenage girls would put a piece of lead in an iron spoon, then melt the lead over the fire and, finally, pour it into cold water. Why? Because the resulting shape might show them what trade their future husbands would have.

Another variation of this was to pour molten lead through the hole of the handle of the key to their front door – straight into cold water. Again, a hoped-for husband's trade could be guessed by the shape.

All sorts of things could be placed under pillows to produce dreams about one's future husband. A sprig of rosemary was popular, and some girls used to take a yew sprig from a graveyard to bed with them. Put under the

Girls tried to discover the trade of their future husbands by dropping molten lead into cold water.

pillow, it, too, might produce a result.

Others believe that Halloween is the right time to consult a fortune-teller, hoping that on this strange night a tall or short, dark or fair, stranger may be spotted – in the cards, on the palm, or even in tea leaves.

Halloween was once called Nut Crack Night in the north of England. A boy and a girl would each put a hazelnut on a fire and think of each other, saying, "If he (or she) loves me, pop and fly; if he (or she) hates me, lie and die."

Another nut game predicts the very opposite. If the nuts burn to ashes, a happy marriage is in store for the couple; but if the nuts burst in the flames, it means that things will not be so good.

Games to do with putting hazelnuts on a fire were popular at Halloween.

A Feast of Apples

The apple is the most important of all the fruits and plants at Halloween. This is not just because of the games that people play with them – some are described on page 42. Apples were once thought to be a link between men and the gods.

The druids believed in an apple land called Avalon, which was where the immortals lived. Immortal souls had to pass through water to get there. Our link with that fabled past – ducking in water for apples at Halloween – is not so romantic!.

Not that you always have to bob for apples. In England, just eating certain apples, called Allens, is believed to bring good luck. By putting an Allen apple under your pillow, you could dream a wish and eat the apple in the morning. Anyone wishing to live more dangerously can

Apple games have been part of Halloween fun for hundreds of years

28

play the game of eating an apple while balancing on a rod of wood, on which there is also a lighted candle.

Yet another use of apples was to tell fortunes from the peeling. First the apple was peeled so that the peeling stayed in one piece. Then the peel was thrown over the right shoulder. A girl looked down at the peel to see what letter shape it had made on the ground. That was the initial of her future love's name.

In another apple ceremony, the performer brushes or combs his or her hair in front of a mirror at midnight, while eating an apple. Soon the form of the performer's future husband or wife will be reflected in the mirror. This is just an entertaining game now, but in olden days it was taken seriously.

An image of your future partner is supposed to appear in a mirror if you comb your hair at midnight while eating an apple.

The Night for Naughtiness

Mischief Night

In the United States, Halloween night activities have often gotten a little too wild, sometimes ending up with the destruction of property. But even this behavior has its roots in tradition. In some parts of northern England, Halloween used to be called Mischief Night.

Taking doors off their hinges seems to have been a particularly popular Halloween pastime. Sometimes the doors were thrown into ponds or dumped miles from the scene of the crime. Other times, farmers would awake to find their wagon on the top of the barn roof, thanks to some mischief makers. The day after Mischief Night was a miserable time for many people, and no doubt still is in certain places in England!

In the United States, Halloween night usually sees some mischief from groups of teenagers out late at night. Their activities can include anything from throwing eggs at houses and cars (usually the property of people the mischief

Taking doors off their hinges was a popular Mischief Night pastime.

Doors were often dumped far away from the scenes of the crimes.

makers know!) to taking jack-o'-lanterns from outside houses and destroying them in the streets. Although the handiwork of these mischief makers often creates a mess that must be cleaned up the next day, they are usually not destructive.

Fortunately, though, most people enjoy Halloween without making any mischief.

More Mischief

In Scotland, high jinks on Mischief Night were allowed to continue for much longer than anywhere else in Britain.

A good game on the night was to climb onto a roof and pile turf into the chimney top. That was a sure way to fill a house with smoke, since the smoke from the fireplace could not get out of the chimney and was forced back into the

A chimney full of turf was one prank you could expect if you lived in Scotland.

house. At that time, most people heated their home with a fire. Fortunately, the chances of a smoke-filled house are less because few people now have real fires.

Smashing bottles was fun, too, just beneath a window. The owners naturally thought that the window had been smashed, but by the time they appeared, the mischief makers were off to do the same again elsewhere.

If you got angry at the tricksters, you were likely to be tormented far more on the next Mischief Night. So it was best to accept their mischief in good humor.

Scottish children had extra fun during the early 1900s on Mischief Night. They bombarded doors with turnips and cabbages, and removed farming implements from farms. Irish children did the same. Many a farmer had to look for his plow, even his cart, on November 1, All Saints' Day. It must have seemed like "All Sinners' Day" to them.

On Mischief Night, Irish and Scottish children used to bombard doors with turnips and cabbages.

33

Guisers used to put on masks or blackened their faces before roaming parishes demanding money or food.

The Guisers

Guisers, or guizers, are Halloween characters that have a very long history. They also originated in Great Britain. "Guiser" is short for "disguiser," and disguising yourself is a sensible precaution when you are playing pranks on people. Some say the guises go back to ancient druid days. Then, the druids blackened their faces for protection with the ashes of a bonfire.

Guising was done by young men and women. They roamed parishes, wearing masks or soot-blackened faces, and they demanded money or food. In the last century, they improved their image by coming indoors and entertaining people by singing and acting. The guisers were likely to appear at other festivals,

34

and people treated them very well so they would not come back for another year.

Guisers used to sing songs about apples and strong beer, a good tactic to get the householder to give them enough strong drink to appease or satisfy them for a year.

Guising lives on in the custom of trick-or-treating. The old-time guisers carried the turnip masks and lanterns associated with Halloween. Today we use pumpkins instead of turnips.

The Halloween masks link our present festival with Samhain and the masked dances that took place in ancient times. Up to a century ago, Scotland guisers looked quite frightening in some areas. The men masked or blackened their faces supposedly to hide them from the dead. It also prevented the living from knowing who was playing pranks on them.

A pumpkin is being hollowed out to make a lantern.

Magic Lanterns

Hinton St. George, a village in England, has a fine-sounding name, and also a fine old Halloween custom. In fact, its great night falls on the last Thursday in October every year, which is only sometimes October 31. Yet it ranks as one of the most important of all Halloween festivals.

For the village has a festival of "punkies," and the villagers regard Halloween as Punky Night.

The punkies are Halloween lanterns made from mangel-wurzels, a large type of beet, which cattle eat. They hollow them out for the big occasion. Then the candles are put inside the punkies.

These lanterns date back at least to the 1840s. It began one Halloween when the village women were becoming worried that their men had not returned home from the fields. The men had

Pumpkins like this one are made into lanterns at Halloween.

A group of children from Hinton St. George with their punkies.

all the lanterns with them, so the women decided to make some out of mangel-wurzels. From that time on, punkies were made every Halloween. Many were marvelous to look at, so cleverly were they designed.

Today, the children of Hinton St. George design and make their own punkies, then parade around the village with them, singing and knocking at doors. They hope to be given a new candle or a coin for their song. As they go around the village, the children sing:

It's Punkie Night tonight.
Give us a candle, give us a light,
If you don't, you'll get a fright.

It's Punkie Night tonight.
Adam and Eve, they'd never believe
It's Punkie Night tonight.

Halloween Today

The Puritan Past

When people leave home to settle in other countries, they naturally like to take happy reminders of their old life with them. That is what the English, Scottish, Irish and Welsh settlers did when they crossed the Atlantic to North America from the 1600s on.

Yet it was not until the last century that Halloween became a popular festival in America. Many of the early settlers were Puritans, and they had very strict religious beliefs. To them, Halloween was a heathen event and the work of the devil. That ruled out all kinds of Halloween celebrations completely.

America's early settlers did not celebrate Halloween.

In the last century, the Irish and Scots immigrants brought renewed interest in Halloween to America.

In the 1800s, things started to change. The Irish and Scots, who came in large numbers, did not leave Halloween behind them. They brought all their favorite traditions, which soon caught on throughout the United States and Canada. People began playing tricks on one another and blaming them on goblins. It was all in the spirit of Halloween.

It's hard to say exactly how or when people first began giving out treats to keep from being tricked. Even before the practice of trick-or-treating became popular, children were dressing up in masks and costumes on Halloween night. Soon people were handing out treats to the costumed creatures.

Trick or Treat!

Trick-or-treating is the highlight of Halloween for most American and Canadian children. They usually dress up in a mask and costume and go from door to door in groups shouting "Trick or treat!" Very young children are accompanied by an adult, who usually waits in the shadows while the youngster is at the door.

Although people used to give treats to avoid being tricked or frightened, today they give them just for the fun of it. Very few modern trick-or-treaters play tricks. Instead, they just try to collect as many goodies as they can. Most people give candy, but some give pennies or other small change, and others give fruit or a health snack.

Instead of collecting candy on Halloween night, some children collect money for the United Nations Children's Fund, or UNICEF. That way, they can have fun and at the same time help children all around the world.

Jack-o'-lanterns are an important part of Halloween. The pumpkin is hollowed out and then carved, usually with a spooky face. Then a candle is put inside to give the face an eerie glow. On the night of Halloween, jack-o'-lanterns can be seen looking out of the windows of many houses and apartments after dark.

Jack-o'-lanterns got their name from a fellow named Jack who, according to an old Irish legend, was so stingy with his money that he was

A dummy and some pumpkin lanterns made especially for the Halloween celebrations.

not allowed into heaven. But poor Jack had played pranks on the devil, so he was not allowed into hell, either! Instead, he is destined to wander around forever, with his lantern, waiting for Judgment Day.

Dressing up is very much a part of trick-or-treating.

Halloween Games

The most famous Halloween party games involve apples. This is a direct throwback to the Roman festival of Pomona, the goddess of trees and fruit, mentioned on page 13.

One traditional game is bobbing for apples, and although it is messy, it is still played at many Halloween gatherings. A large tub is filled with water and a dozen apples or so. One at a time, players put their heads in the tub and try to grab an apple with their teeth. It may sound easy, but it isn't. More than likely, everyone will get soaking wet in the process of getting the apples. The game continues, as well as the soakings, until each person has had a turn or all the apples are gone. A coin is sometimes stuck in each apple as a prize.

Thanks to the Roman goddess, Pomona, apple games are played at Halloween.

Like bobbing for apples, snap apple is a game that immigrants from England, Scotland, Wales and Ireland brought with them. Apples are hung on strings from the ceiling or a wooden beam, and players must grab the apples with their teeth. The apples swing away more often than they are caught.

Another game played with apples is purely American. The players form two lines, and the object of the game is to pass an apple down each line from under one chin to under the next chin. Players cannot use their hands, and they must not drop the apple. Whichever team finishes first wins the game.

Snap apple is a fun game that can be played by everyone.

43

Happy Halloween

As we have seen, Halloween is a strange mixture of opposites. People are concerned with the past and with the spirits and ghosts of the dead, but at the same time they are just as concerned with finding out about the future. It's a night to play pranks – and to be deliciously scared.

Today the celebration of Halloween may be just for fun, but it's easy to understand why our ancestors thought otherwise. With Halloween came the dark months of the year, when it seemed natural that fearful creatures would be at large. There were witches. . .

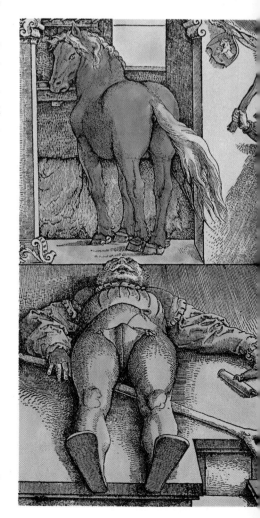

> Hey-how for Halloween!
> All the witches to be seen,
> Some in black and some in green,
> Hey-how for Halloween.

. . . and there were ghosts:

> She haunts the house,
> She haunts the green,
> And glowers on me
> With her wild-cat e'en.

Frightening stories of witchcraft and evil spirits were very much a part of Halloween in the past.

"E'en" means eyes, and some of our ancestors must have kept their eyes wide open at Halloween, if only to find the quickest way home.

These days Halloween is something to look forward to for weeks ahead of time, as children – and some adults, too – decide what they will "be" on Halloween. Although some trick-or-treaters carry plastic jack-o'-lanterns for collecting their treats, many now carry large pillowcases or shopping bags in hopes of Halloween filled with lots of treats.

Today, Halloween is a time for dressing up, taking part in games and having fun.

Glossary

Celts A group of people who inhabited most of Europe in pre-Roman times.

Druid A priest of the ancient Celts.

Enchanted Under the power of spells.

Fabled Something made famous in a story or legend about mythical characters or events.

Fortune-teller A person who makes predictions about the future by looking into a crystal ball, reading palms or playing cards.

Heathen A person who is not a Christian, Jew or Muslim.

High jinks Lively enjoyment.

Immortal Something that lives forever or is never forgotten.

Mischief Night A night, traditionally at Halloween, on which people play annoying tricks on others.

Pagan Another word for heathen.

Phantom A ghost or ghost-like figure.

Samhain A Celtic festival giving thanks for the harvest at the end of the year.

Superstition A misguided belief in magic and charms.

Warlock A male witch.

Will-o'-the-wisp A person or thing that is elusive or misleads.

Further Reading

If you would like to read more about Halloween and Halloween activities look for the following books:

The Scary Halloween Costume Book by Carol Barkin and Elizabeth James (Lothrop, 1983)

Witches, Pumpkins, and Grinning Ghosts by Edna Barth (Seabury, 1972)

Halloween Fun by Judith H. Corwin (Messner, 1983)

The All-Around Pumpkin Book by Margery Cuyler (Holt, 1980)

Halloween by D.J. Herda (Watts, 1983)

Index

Acknowledgments

The publisher would like to thank all those who provided pictures on the following pages: Mary Evans Picture Library cover, 4, 5, 12, 13, 15, 16, 19,22, 26, 27, 38, 39, 42; Sally & Richard Greenhill 11, 23, 35, 36,40; Outlook Films Ltd. 10; PHOTRI 45; Ronald Sheridan's Photo-Library 44; Malcolm S. Walker 7, 9, 14, 20, 25, 28, 29, 30, 31, 32, 33, 34, 47, 41, 43.

© Copyright 1984 Wayland (Publishers) Ltd.
61 Western Road, Hove, East Sussex
BN3 1JD, England